Come To Me

In The Night Season

VOLUME I

SHAWNA PRINCE

Come To Me

Cover by Reginald Blanks—Christ Like Graphics, Houston, TX

Photographer—Geralda Baugh

ISBN: 0998521909
ISBN 13: 9780998521909

ACKNOWLEDGMENTS

I am honored to share with you the poems of my heart and the encouraging words the Lord shared with me. It is my deepest desire to see all believers persevere through the night season in their life. If it weren't for the grace and mercy of God, I would never have been able to write down these meaningful words that are so dear to my heart.

To God, my Father, and my Lord and Savior, Jesus Christ, without You speaking to me through Your word and comforting me by Your Holy Spirit, I wouldn't have been able to encourage others. On the many nights my eyes filled with tears, and I cried out to You, not understanding the place I was in, You never left me alone; You were always there. I just want to thank You for being there for me during my night seasons. I love You with all my heart. Your daughter always, Shawna.

To Apostle Jerome Nelson Sr. and Pastor Betty Nelson, it is with great honor that I thank you. Since I have been a member of Spirit of Life, you have poured the word of God into me. In a world that needs to see Jesus, you are both true examples of what it means to be a Christian (a disciple indeed).

To Brian, Brittney, Catina, Catherine, Chimyra, Khalilah, Sharon, and Undra, the prayers, support, and encouraging words you gave me while I was writing were truly inspiring. Thank you for believing in me and what the Lord is doing through me.

Thank you to my family and friends for all the encouragement along the way. Without you, none of this would have been possible.

CONTENTS

FOREWORD

I remember when Shawna Prince and her son first came to the church. She was this quiet, demure, very modest young woman that didn't have anything to say – or so we thought. I don't remember hearing her say much more than a few words for a long time. I believe she was going through some of her Holy Spirit training during those first years at the church (some of the things that you'll read in this book).

Then came the day that she was presented to the church to teach her first message. As we listened, how shocked some of us were! She could talk! And she knew the Word! She didn't just recite something she'd heard – she KNEW the Word and she taught with authority.

Since that time, I have come to feel close to Shawna (teachers love teachers, you know). Although we don't talk much, just watching her grow has so blessed me. For instance, she was on the praise dance team a few years back. I don't believe that the Shawna who first arrived at Spirit of Life could have done that, and although she wasn't the most visibly expressive on the team, there was purity and honesty in her dance. She was worshipping her Lord her way – quietly and without fanfare.

When Shawna told me that she had written a book, I was so, so proud of her. I always felt she had a life story to tell that would help guide people to the Lord, but I never dreamed I'd get to hear it (or read it). I'd often wanted to ask her about her history, but didn't want to infringe on her privacy.

As you read this book – if you're alive – this book **will** minister to you. I believe that everyone who reads this book will be changed in some form or another – **if** you take the message to heart. I know I was changed! All you have to do is be open to hear His voice, His direction, His correction, His affirmation, and His love for you.

So, without any further ado – I introduce you to an awesome young woman, Shawna Prince, and her life-changing book, "Come to Me."

Mattie L. Walters

INTRODUCTION

Come to Me. Lay down your life, and come after Me,

And you will be forever changed from the inside out.

I will use you for My glory.

I will shine bright through your life.

The people will see Me in you and you in Me.

Break forth, My child, and shine for Me.

Allow Me to use your life no matter the cost.

Come to Me and get lost in My presence.

Get lost in My ways as you come to Me and pray and seek My face.

Lose all thoughts of your past and your current surroundings.

Simply come to Me.

In a time when hearing God's voice is of the utmost importance, in a season where great things are on the horizon, in a place where God is calling you to Himself so that He can minister to you from His heart, you can trust God to guide you through every season of your life when you just simply come to Him.

If you, like many of us, have experienced hard times, stressful situations, and overwhelming feelings of hopelessness and regret, you know that we often look for an answer or a way out so that the pain can stop, or so that we will be relieved from the stress. *Come to Me* is God beckoning the believer to come to Him in every situation and circumstance.

He speaks so that we are comforted. He gives us His strength in place of our weaknesses. He allows us to call out to Him in the night seasons of our lives. When we are desperate and clinging to hope, He continues to speak to our hearts to let us know that He's there in the midst of our storm.

These writings are from over many years, and this is my story of how God brought me out of many difficult night seasons in my life and how He can and will do the same for you.

Allow the Lord to minister to you through these words, poems, and scriptures to lead you to comfort, healing, restoration, and greater trust in God. I pray that you will hear God speaking through these words so that you are encouraged and empowered to live this life for Him.

Chapter 1

Come To Me All Who Are Weary

Mathew 11:28

Come to Me, all who are weary and heavily burdened [by religious rituals that provide no peace], and I will give you rest [refreshing your souls with salvation].

THE FATHER SPEAKS

Come to Me, all who are weary, and I will give you rest. Come to Me, all those who feel unworthy, and I will show you My faithfulness. I am doing a new thing; can you not see it? I am moving by My spirit; can you not perceive it? I love you with an everlasting love; do you not know it? You are Mine, and I am yours. Rest, trust, and believe that I have you; I am your canopy. I will protect you from the arrow by day and the pestilence by night. I will keep you safe. I redeem you from the hands of the enemy. I speak and declare over you your destiny. For I know the plans and thoughts I have for you, plans for peace and wellbeing and not for disaster, to give you a future and a hope.

Come to Me, and know Me in the fellowship of my suffering.

Come after Me, and sing praises to Me.

I am supreme; I am king; I Am that I Am.

There is no other God besides Me.

Lay down your life, and worship Me.

Sometimes, we as believers become weary. As listed in Merriam-Webster, this means "exhausted in strength, endurance, vigor, or freshness, or having one's patience, tolerance, or pleasure exhausted." Matthew 11:28 states, "Come to Me, all who are weary and heavily burdened [by religious rituals that provide no peace], and I will give you rest [refreshing your souls with salvation]." Also, in Psalm 55:22 it states, to "cast thy burden upon the Lord, [release it,] and He will sustain and uphold you; He will never allow the righteous to be shaken (slip, fall, fail)." During these seasons of weariness, the Lord is asking us to come to Him, and He will give us rest.

He wants us to cast our burden upon Him. I love when the word says "release it," because sometimes we hold on to things that God is asking us to release to Him. We often think that if we hold on to it we can figure something out, but in reality that is what is making us weary, because we are holding on to it. No matter what "it" is, God is asking us to release it – no matter the pain, the unforgiveness, the hurt, and turmoil, or the rejection from others.

Let it go and cry it out. Tell the Lord, "Here! I don't want it any longer; I don't want to hold anything back from You. You, oh Lord, can have it." Remember that no matter what it is, begin to release it to Him and Him alone, for He knows you. He created you and knows your innermost parts. He knows when you're insecure. He knows when you are fearful. He knows when you are prideful, and He knows when you are truly humbled. He knows you, and you can't hide anything from Him, so just come to Him and let Him fix it. Let Him fight for you. Let Him take care of it, because it is too much for you to handle.

It's slowly killing you. Once you release it, you will have a newfound joy in Him. One area I had to release to the Lord was my finances. This is just one of many areas I had to learn to release. For so long I had very little. The Lord wanted to release more to me, but I had no concept of that. I was afraid that if I released it, I would not have enough money to take care of me and my son. Nothing could have been further from the truth.

This scripture is very true: "There is one who scatters, yet increases more; And there is one who withholds more than is right, But it leads to poverty" (Proverbs 11:24). Once I began to let go of my fears of not having enough, I began to see the Lord move on my behalf like never before. It was this thing called "favor" that money could not buy. I remember when I went to buy my first car, they wanted a down payment of $1,100, but I did not have that kind of money. So I figured that I would not be able to purchase it that day. I told the man that I would be back when I had the down payment, which would be in about two to three weeks.

The finance guy said, "OK, that's fine," and left the room, but the salesman came to me and said, "Do you really want this car?"

I answered, "Yes, I do."

He said, "And you will have the money in two to three weeks?"

"Yes, I should have it by then."

Then he said, "I know I should not do this, but I am. There is something about you that I trust, so I am going to pay for your down payment from my personal account."

"No, sir, please don't," I replied. "I will be back in a couple of weeks to pay the down payment."

He said, "But I can't guarantee that the car will still be here for you."

So I thought about it and said OK, and he called the finance guy to come back in the room and handed him the money. The finance guy looked at him and said, "Are you sure that you want to do this?" The guy said yes. Now, this man did not know me, and I surely did not know him, but the Lord saw my need, and I walked out of the dealership that day with keys in hand and drove around town.

Of course, I did go back in a couple of weeks and give him his money back, but God knew that I needed the car to get to work, get to church, and pick up my son during that time. Since then the Lord allowed me to pay off my car early, which was a great blessing. There is a great scripture we need to live by in Matthew 6:2–3 which says, "So whenever you give to the poor and do acts of kindness, do not blow a trumpet before you [to advertise it], as the hypocrites do [like actors acting out a role] in the synagogues and in the streets, so that they may be honored and recognized and praised by men."

"I assure you and most solemnly say to you, they [already] have their reward in full. But when you give to the poor and do acts of kindness, do not let your left hand know what your right hand is doing [give in complete secrecy]." God has truly blessed my life because of this practice. When I finally realized that there is a scripture that really will help you through every situation that you go through, it became much easier to release my cares and burdens to Him. Once I released the cares of my finances to Him, He began to speak to me about giving. I am only sharing this story in hopes that you will see how God turned my situation around, and now I have the opportunity to give.

My mom and I went out to breakfast one morning. As we were sitting there eating, I began to look around the restaurant. My eyes fell on two older ladies. Then the Lord spoke and said to pay for their meal.

I was nervous, because what if it was just me and not the Lord? Well, I could not rest until I said, "Yes, Lord." So I got up and went to the cashier and asked for their waiter so that I could pay for their meal. I paid for it and told the waiter not to tell the ladies who had paid. I went and sat back down. As it turned out, the ladies asked the waiter who had paid for their food, and the waiter pointed at me. At first I was upset, because I had asked the waiter not to say anything. But God needed it to happen.

So about ten minutes later, the two ladies came over to me, and one said, "Excuse us, but why did you pay for our meal?"

I said, "Because the Lord told me to."

Then she smiled and said, "I know He cares, because this is our first morning back into town since we were displaced by the hurricane, and this is our first meal. Thank you; this really did make our day." This showed me that God really does care about His people, and He will take care of us. We must lay down our burdens and cast our cares on Him. For He truly does care for us.

NOT FORSAKEN

God, You knew me before I was born;

You loved me before I said a word.

You are my lover; You are my friend.

You are my everlasting Father.

You are all I need; You're forever with me.

You are all knowing; You are my peace.

Sometimes I lie in my bed at night and cry

and wonder why it is so hard to live this life.

But I am comforted by You in that Your love is forever true;

You're pure and holy, and what You speak

to my heart calms all my fears. You are forever near;

You are, You are,

You are, You are,

You are the great I Am.

To My Beloved

To those who feel abandoned, Lord, I see You reaching down with Your outstretched arms, letting them know that they are not alone. I see You bringing them close to Your bosom for protection. I see you caring for them like a Father tends and cares for his child.

"Not abandoned," I hear the Lord shouting, but oh, so close to Him and loved by the Father.

Scriptures for Reflection

Galatians 6:9

And let us not be weary in well doing: for in due season we shall reap, if we faint not. (KJV)

2 Corinthians 12:9-10

[9]And he said unto me, My grace is sufficient for thee: for my strength is made perfect in weakness. Most gladly therefore will I rather glory in my infirmities, that the power of Christ may rest upon me. [10]Therefore I take pleasure in infirmities, in reproaches, in necessities, in persecutions, in distresses for Christ's sake: for when I am weak, then am I strong. (KJV)

Ephesians 6:10-17

[10] Finally, my brethren, be strong in the Lord, and in the power of his might. [11]Put on the whole armour of God, that ye may be able to stand against the wiles of the devil. [12]For we wrestle not against flesh and blood, but against principalities, against powers, against the rulers of the darkness of this world, against spiritual wickedness in high places. [13]Wherefore take unto you the whole armour of God, that ye may be able to withstand in the evil day, and having done all, to stand. [14]Stand therefore, having your loins girt about with truth, and having on the breastplate of righteousness; [15]And your feet shod with the preparation of the gospel of peace; [16]Above all, taking the shield of faith, wherewith ye shall be able to quench all the fiery darts of the wicked. [17]And take the helmet of salvation, and the sword of the Spirit, which is the word of God: (KJV)

Chapter 2

Come To Me And Rest

Hebrews 4:1-9

Let us therefore fear, lest, a promise being left us of entering into his rest, any of you should seem to come short of it. ^{2}For unto us was the gospel preached, as well as unto them: but the word preached did not profit them, not being mixed with faith in them that heard it. ^{3}For we which have believed do enter into rest, as he said, As I have sworn in my wrath, if they shall enter into my rest: although the works were finished from the foundation of the world. ^{4}For he spake in a certain place of the seventh day on this wise, And God did rest the seventh day from all his works. ^{5}And in this place again, If they shall enter into my rest. ^{6}Seeing therefore it remaineth that some must enter therein, and they to whom it was first preached entered not in because of unbelief: ^{7}Again, he limiteth a certain day, saying in David, To day, after so long a time; as it is said, To day if ye will hear his voice, harden not your hearts. ^{8}For if Jesus had given them rest, then would he not afterward have spoken of another day. ^{9}There remaineth therefore a rest to the people of God. (KJV)

THE FATHER SPEAKS

Come to Me and rest. Learn of Me and My ways;

My yoke is easy, and My burden is light.

Release all worry and anxiety.

Meditate on My word day and night.

Be strengthened; be built up with My word.

I am bigger than your circumstances.

Know that I am He that delivers and sets free.

I surround you with My ministering angels.

Now worship Me in the beauty of holiness.

Lay prostrate before Me and rest.

Let My presence restore you, and let my presence refresh you.

Allow Me to fill your cup to overflowing.

Take a deep breath…exhale…and rest!

ome to Me and rest...easier said than done, right? I know from experience, but I realize as time goes on that the more I choose to rest and allow God to move on my behalf, the more peace I experience. When God said there is a rest to the people of God, it was because He had already established promises to us. Hebrews chapter 4 talks about the children of Israel not entering into God's rest. He had already planned for the children of Israel to enter the promised land, but because of murmuring and complaining, they didn't enter it.

What! They didn't enter into rest because of unbelief, not taking God at His word, not relying on Him to bring it to pass, but instead being rebellious and stubborn and unbelieving. I choose to receive God's rest for my life and choose to rest from my own work just as God rested from His. I choose to walk in the promises of God that He spoke over my life. He is saying it's time to receive His rest for your life. It is already established; it has already been spoken by the Creator, so enter His rest for you.

In the night season, the rest of God may seem unattainable because of all the walls that seem like they are caving in around you. Do know that the rest of God is here for you. Remember that He has already established your promises. Choose to believe, and rest in knowing that this is not the end, even though you are going through tough times right now.

HOLDING ON

I'm going to be a faithful servant unto You.

I'm going to hold on until You bless me.

I promise I am going to hold on to You.

Though trials may come in my life,

and the way may seem dark,

I know You will see me through.

Prayer

No More Worries

Lord, I pray for those experiencing anxiety and worry. Your word says not to worry about what they will eat or drink or how they will put clothes on their backs; not to worry about tomorrow, for tomorrow will take care of itself. Lord, I ask that every need is supplied for them.

For You said in Your word that You will supply all our needs according to Your riches in Glory. Where they are being presumptuous, I ask that You remove it. Where their minds keep wondering how and when You are going to fix it, I ask that it ceases.

Let the word speak in their situations. For Lord, You said, "Be anxious for nothing but in everything, by prayer and supplication, make your request made known to God." I ask that they release it now and truly trust You for their provision, trust that You will provide a way in their situation.

You will show Your power and move on their behalf. You are not a God that sleeps. You are not a God Who does not understand, but You want to move for Your children.

You want to show grace in their weakness. Even though they did not do everything right, You still want to move on their behalves. Let them know and understand, in Jesus name. Amen.

Scriptures for Reflection

Psalm 62:7

On God my salvation and my glory rest; He is my rock of [unyielding] strength, my refuge is in God.

Psalm 116:7

Return to your rest, O my soul, for the Lord has dealt bountifully with you.

Psalm 132:14

This is my rest forever: here will I dwell; for I have desired it.

Chapter 3

Come To Me And I Will Speak Peace

John 14:27

Peace I leave with you; My [perfect] peace I give to you; not as the world gives do I give to you. Do not let your heart be troubled, nor let it be afraid. [Let My perfect peace calm you in every circumstance and give you courage and strength for every challenge.]

THE FATHER SPEAKS

Come to Me, and I will speak peace over you.

The turmoil within will cease to be.

I love you with an everlasting love.

Come to Me, and I will give you rest in the night season.

You will rest in fields of green grass,

and I will lead you to pools of fresh water. For I Am your hiding place.

I Am your great shepherd;

I Am forever with you.

Know that in Me is everything you need.

Strength, health, wealth, peace, love, joy—

all these things are in Me and belong to you.

Know that I love you and care about you.

I see you right where you are.

Even to your old age, I Am He,

and even to hair white with age will I carry you.

I have made, and I will bear;

Yes, I will carry and will save you.

J esus said, "Peace I leave with you; [perfect] peace I give to you; not as the world gives do I give to you. Do not let your heart be troubled, nor let it be afraid. [Let My perfect peace calm you in every circumstance and give you courage and strength for every challenge.]" (John 14:27). During the season of great rejection, with people talking about me behind my back, and family and so-called friends walking away, I had to lean and depend on the peace of God.

It hurt tremendously, and I didn't even know why it had to happen this way, but only God knew the nights I cried to Him about the rejection and how I felt mistreated. Then He reminded me of how He was mistreated and betrayed—talked about and misunderstood - and He was the Son of God. His word says, "Yea, and all that will live godly in Christ Jesus shall suffer persecution."

So when people lie about you and slander your name until people around you start to look at you differently because they listened to what other people had to say about you, don't even fret. Just know this also happened to Jesus, and we are no greater than our teacher. During this process I had to learn how to forgive people for the mistakes they were making in gossiping about me and spreading lies.

This was so hard, because it's one thing if it's true, but it's another thing when it's a lie. I really had to go to God each and every day and give it to Him. Anger would rise up inside me, and I wanted to defend myself. But He wouldn't let me, and the tears ran down my cheeks, because I couldn't say anything to anyone. I wanted to shout from the mountaintops, "Listen to me when I tell you they are lying about me." But I had to suffer through it, because God was doing something down on the inside of me. He wanted to know, "When they talk about you, when they hate you, when they ignore you and reject you, will you still serve Me?"

He was growing me up so that I could begin to pray and love my enemies, do good to them who hated me, bless them who cursed me, and pray for them who despitefully used me. I had to submit to the truth of His word.

I would be lying if I said that it was easy and that it felt great to do this. I would begin to pray for them when I was not feeling like it at all. But something would happen in the midst of my praying - my heart began to soften, and the tears that were falling at first because I felt hurt and betrayed began to be tears for them, because God would begin to show me that they did not know what they were doing. They were hurting too, and they had issues that they never dealt with, so in turn they were hurting me without even realizing it. In the midst of all this, His peace was still speaking over me.

KEEP GOING ON

The road may be long and hard.

The sun may never seem to shine.

You might keep failing in everything you do.

But there is someone watching you, and

He still loves you, so keep going on.

It may seem like no one cares,

but God will always be there.

You still have a long way to go;

you can make it if you try.

When you make it, don't turn back;

look at where you are, and keep going on.

The Response from the Beloved

Your peace, oh Lord, surrounds me. The stillness quiets my soul. Your perspective increases in my thoughts. Your love carries me through. The pain that was once so great is now diminished to just a memory, a slideshow of my past. Lord, I thank You for deliverance.

Lord, I praise You for Your faithfulness. Lord, I bless You with all that is within me. Bless Your holy name. Be pleased with my life. Be glorified in my life. Use me for Your glory. For it is for You and You alone that I live and breathe. For it is for You and You alone that I die.

You are my rock and my salvation; of whom shall I be afraid? You are the strength of my life; whom shall I fear? Though a thousand die at my right hand and ten thousand at my left hand, I will not fear, for Thou art with me. You shine Your light in my darkness so that I can see the path to take.

You come in and overtake my worries, fears, and anxieties, and You tell them to cease. You breathe new life into me. You truly are the restorer of my soul.

Scriptures for Reflection

Isaiah 26:3

"You will keep in perfect *and* constant peace *the one* whose mind is steadfast [that is, committed and focused on You—in both inclination and character], Because he trusts *and* takes refuge in You [with hope and confident expectation].

Jeremiah 29:11

For I know the thoughts that I think toward you, saith the Lord, thoughts of peace, and not of evil, to give you an expected end. (KJV)

Numbers 6:26

The LORD lift up His countenance (face) upon you [with divine approval], And give you peace [a tranquil heart and life].'

Chapter 4

Come To Me And Don't Wait On A Feeling

Proverbs 8:17

I love those who love me;
And those who seek me early *and* diligently will find me.

THE FATHER SPEAKS

Come to Me and don't wait on a feeling or an unction.

I will meet you when you come.

Just come to Me, and I will meet you in the run.

Know that I care for you and love you forever

…and…ever…and…ever and ever with My everlasting love.

Just come and sit at My feet…

Lie prostrate before Me with your arms outstretched, saying,

"Abba Father, heal me,

Purge me, cleanse me, wash me, and make me whole."

Know this day that I am God sitting on the throne.

I will wash over your sins like the ocean, and they will be washed away, never to be remembered again.

They will be removed as far as the east is from the west.

Trust Me and come to Me, and

I will make you whole.

In some of our night seasons, we have to face our past and the things that we did wrong. We have to ask the Lord for forgiveness for how we treated people or for the sins we have done, learn how to forgive ourselves for the mistakes we made, and accept God's grace and mercy for our lives. The enemy loves to keep God's people in condemnation, because it keeps us from moving forward in God. This process can sometimes take weeks, months, or even years.

Sometimes we wait for a feeling or unction from the Lord before we go to Him and seek Him. He is saying not to wait for a feeling, because you can find Him without a feeling. He just needs you to come to Him and seek out His will and His way of doing things. It took me many years to understand that I didn't have to feel a certain way before I could go and spend time with Him. Every time I made the effort, He would meet me there.

Every time I chose to silence my phone, turn off the TV, and remove myself from people and go into my private dwelling place, He would be there waiting with all His fullness. Every time would be different, but He would blow my mind with His words and with His presence. We have to get out of this religious thing where we come to God a certain way. To be honest, He just wants you to come; it's as easy as that.

Go and sit with him with no distractions, where you can focus only on Him. I promise you that He will come in and overtake you with His goodness. God is looking at your heart, not the things you have done for Him. Were your motives pure when you did this or that?

Did you do it to be seen by men, or did you do it to please the Father because He asked you to?

When you come to Him and begin to seek Him out, He will begin to reveal all that He is, and He will begin to shine the light on any darkness inside you, the places you may not have wanted to see or just didn't know were there. He does it because He loves us, and He does not want His children walking in error or deception. I remember one time when I was spending time with Him, and He showed me there was fear, pride, worry, disobedience, laziness, selfishness, and an unteachable spirit in my heart.

I cried because I didn't want those things interfering with my relationship with Him, and I just wanted to please God. So I agreed with what He showed me and began to let Him work those things out of my heart. I began to pray and ask for forgiveness and asked Him to wash me clean. The more I went to Him with these things, the more He would give me a scripture to live by so that I wouldn't fall into these areas so easily.

Do know, however, that it's still a choice to live by the word or not. You have to choose to walk this word out every day and not every other day. I just had to say that, because sometimes I think we listen to people and what they have gone through and think that it happened overnight. But this was and is a process every day. One of my favorite scriptures in the whole wide world is, "And Enoch walked with God: and he was not; for God took him (Genesis 5:24 [KJV])." Hebrews 11:5 says, "By faith Enoch was translated that he should not see death;

and was not found, because God had translated him: for before his translation he had this testimony, that he pleased God."

To be able to say that I walked with God to a degree that I pleased him so much that He would just take me off the planet—that speaks volumes to me. I want to seek God out in His ways so that I please Him in everything that I do and say. Yes, this will cause you to die to your own will, and your own way, and your flesh will fight it, because it does not like death. But the more you die, the more your spirit will soar. There is a scripture that talks about seeking God in Isaiah 45:19. It states, "I have not spoken in secret, in a corner of a land of darkness; I did not say to the descendants of Jacob, 'Seek Me in vain [with no benefit for yourselves].' I, the Lord, speak righteousness [the truth-trustworthy, a straightforward correlation between deeds and words], Declaring things that are upright."

An area I see that many people struggle with is forgiving themselves for the past sins they committed. I struggled with this for many years, not able to receive the forgiveness of God. I felt like certain past sins were too big for God to forgive. And in essence, I would hold myself captive for these sins. But over the years, He has shown me that this is far from the truth. He showed me that He paid the full price for this. My sins He remembers no more.

One area I especially struggled with was having sex at an early age and having a baby out of wedlock in my teenage years. I struggled with the shame and guilt of this for many years, well into my twenties, until I received God's forgiveness in this area of my life. Then I was able to forgive myself - meaning realizing and accepting what I had done and receiving God's grace and mercy, which in return gave me gratitude for Jesus and all that He did by dying for my sins. I remember one night I was writing, and the Lord began to give me a burden for those who had an abortion. I never experienced this personally, but I know of many people who have done this and are still stuck with the guilt and shame of it. I began to weep and cry, and I began to write. It was like I had gone through the experience myself.

He was letting me feel how they felt, all the guilt and shame that they carried, and I began to pray for them and write a poem entitled "I Will Never Forget." Please know that the enemy tries to remind us of who we used to be, but God reminds us of who we are in Him. Be encouraged. All you have to do is repent and turn from your wicked ways, and He will forgive you.

He will wash you clean as if you had never done it, because you are covered by the blood of Jesus. Imagine a blank white piece of paper, and begin to see all your sins on it. Then see someone taking a thick can of red paint and pouring it on the paper. The red paint covers all the sins that are on the paper. This is what Jesus did for us on the cross. He took our sins and covered them with His blood. When God the Father looks at us, He sees only the blood of Jesus and He no longer sees our sins.

I will never forget

the hurt, the pain, the disgrace, and the shame—

the laughter I will never hear—

and I will never get to wipe away those tears.

The family, the friends,

God and His love,

the little fingers, the little toes,

and the little button nose

that I will never get to touch

or feel, and I will never get to hold you close or hold you so near.

If you can hear me now,

I want you to never forget,

like flowers never forget to blossom,

but remember, you will always be here in my heart.

I love you more than you will ever know.

I listened to family and friends

when I should have listened to my beating and natural heart.

I know God's grace will carry me through,

even if it does not seem like it after that painful day I aborted you.

STAY FREE

Me, You, whoever knew

that one day You would deliver me from me.

You know that I finally realized that

we all have messed up somehow or another.

The hardest part is accepting what I've done and moving on.

I just want to be clean and pure in my body,

in my mind, and in my spirit.

Lord, please make me over so that I can walk out this life for You.

As I walk out of the chains and ropes from my past,

I hear a voice that says, "Stay free; don't go back."

We have a choice every day that we are alive

to either live for Christ or die.

Because every day you go without Christ being first

a little of you dies inside day by day.

As I sit here tonight, as I cry, I say to myself, "Stay free."

To My Beloved

My grace is sufficient for thee. In your weakness I make you strong with My strength. My grace is on the path of your life. I move for you with My grace.

You shall continue in My grace. Grace is there when you sleep at night and when you wake up in the morning. It's there in your darkest hour.

When you feel like you will be consumed by the fire and when you feel like you can't make it another day, My grace is there to carry you through. My grace is for you.

Scriptures for Reflection

Psalm 103:12

As far as the east is from the west, So far has He removed our transgressions from us. (KJV)

Micah 7:19

He shall again have compassion on us; He will subdue *and* tread underfoot our wickedness [destroying sin's power]. Yes, You will cast all our sins Into the depths of the sea.

1 John 1:9

If we [freely] admit that we have sinned *and* confess our sins, He is faithful and just [true to His own nature and promises], and will forgive our sins and cleanse us *continually* from all unrighteousness [our wrongdoing, everything not in conformity with His will and purpose].

Isaiah 38:17

"Indeed, it was for my own well-being that I had such bitterness; But You have loved back my life from the pit of nothingness (destruction), For You have cast all my sins behind Your back.

Chapter 5

Come To Me When Your Way Seems Strange

Psalm 1:6

For the LORD knows *and* fully approves the way of the righteous,
But the way of the wicked shall perish.

THE FATHER SPEAKS

Come to Me when your way seems strange.

I am your way, I am your truth, and I am your life.

If I be for you, who can be against you?

Let Me fight your battles.

I am strong in your weakness.

I am able to do abundantly more than you can ask or think.

Trust Me even in this.

Let Me change your perspective on the situation.

In Me you can do anything.

Come to Me with your whole heart, holding nothing back.

Let Me have My way,

Releasing you from your past sins, regret, and unfaithfulness.

Let Me come in and overwhelm you with My love.

Trust your Father, Your God,

Your Daddy,

Your King,

One day while I was driving I began to express how I felt. I began to say, *Can you hear me? Can you hear me? What would you hear me say? Would you hear what you wanted to hear, or would you hear what's on my heart today? I've been molested and abused and so many times confused…some days not wanting to live. So I look in the mirror and see the reflection that comes back at me. I look and see what lies deep within. Deep down and buried away so deep that I forgot its name. Shame, fear, regret, and unforgiveness toward myself.*

God wants to heal that place that you have locked away. Lord, begin to change the inner man. Begin to remove all wickedness and all iniquities. Let purity reign in my members again.

As a child, I did not understand what was happening to me. I did not know the weight I would carry all the way into my twenties; I did not know that pornography, masturbation, and fornication would be a part of me well into my adulthood; I did not know I was bound, until one day my whole world came crashing down. I was in college, part of a gospel choir, and we went out of town as usual to sing and celebrate with another choir for their anniversary.

Like many times before, they had a guest speaker come and minister, but this time was different. The man of God stood up and began to tell his testimony of how he grew up and was shot several times. Then he went on to tell us how he was molested. This struck a big chord in my heart, as I had buried the memories from my past so that I could function in life. I remember when I was thirteen and I wanted to commit suicide. I knew that I could not keep living if I had the memories keep playing in my head. So I told myself that I would never again think about what happened to me, because the memories and the pain were too much for me to bear. So somehow I convinced myself that it did not happen. But, as I listened to the speaker on that college trip finish his testimony, he said, "If you were molested, please stand up so I can pray for you."

I never did stand up, because I was crying so heavily, and I was overwhelmed by pain, shame, and fear all at once. On my way back home, a couple of ladies and I were talking, and it turned out they had gone through similar situations, but some were worse than mine. This was the beginning of the process of my healing. I wish I could tell you that the process was quick and easy, but it wasn't. It was very hard and long. I fought God tooth and nail about it, because I didn't understand how God could let that happen to me. So I ran from Him. I ran far and wide, looking for someone – anyone - to stop the massive pain I felt in my heart and soul.

I found myself entangled in relationship after relationship and doing things I thought I would never do. But God in His mercy, grace, and love never stopped pursuing me. Because He knew that I wanted to be healed. He knew that I just wanted and needed the pain to stop. The day came when I stopped running. It was a night when I was fed up with my relationships, I was fed up with myself, and I did not want to live anymore. I sat on the side of my bed and cried out to the Lord. When I say I cried out, I mean I cried out sobbing and could not articulate any words. I began to speak, but they weren't words I understood. It was the Holy Ghost praying. Once I finished, I sat there in the silence of my room and laid back down and went to sleep. The next morning I woke up feeling refreshed, and it felt like total newness had hit my life. I went through the days ahead able to see clearly. The more time I spent with Him, the more He ministered to my heart.

The more He spoke His words of truth over me, the more I became free in Him. I still had nights filled with tears and worry and stress as I walked through the process, but the difference this time was that God was so near. I can't explain how close, but He was really close. He became my true friend, to the point that I would talk to him about any and everything that was on my heart and how I felt. I don't know the moment the healing occurred, but I was no longer depressed. I was no longer angry with the world, and I truly began to love myself.

In my brokenness He began to speak to my heart and encouraged me in the midst of my trouble. He spoke sweet melodies in my surroundings. In my brokenness is where I found His peace. I found His love in the midst of turmoil. He was forever present with me. As I cried out from my heart and as I longed to be close to Him, He drew close to me and healed me from all my wounds and delivered me out of all my trouble. I have to say, I love Him so much. He amazes me. When I think back over my life, only God gets all the glory. I love Him with everything that I am! Allow the Lord to begin to walk you through a process of healing, and letting go of your past hurts.

CHILDHOOD

The meaning of childhood should never be taken for granted.

Childhood is when a child should be playing

instead of calling 911, saying, "Rape."

Childhood is something you should always remember,

instead of trying so hard to fight it way.

Childhood is a time for learning,

not a time for running away.

A time for laughter

but not a time for tears.

Many people say children never have problems as children,

but they should be proud

because they are going to want to go back someday.

One thing they need to ask and understand…

what if the kids don't want to remember

but only want to stay away?

Prayer

Suicidal Thoughts Must Cease and Desist!

Lord, expose the tactics and tricks of the enemy. He is trying to make them abort purpose. I decree and declare now that they will live and not die, to declare the works of the Lord. Peace be still. Every tormenting spirit must leave now, in the name of Jesus. I speak life over my brother and sister right now. I speak life again.

They will begin to have a will to live and a will to fight. Strengthen them even now as I speak, "The joy of the Lord is your strength." They will wait upon You, Lord, and You will renew their strength; they will mount up with wings as eagles; they will run and not be weary; and they will walk and not faint. You will speak, preacher; you will prophesy, prophet; you will win souls, evangelist; you will shepherd His flock, pastor; and you will teach, teacher and minister; you will fulfill your purpose—your calling—your assignment. In Jesus name, amen.

To My Beloved

You belong to Me. You are the child of the King, anointed to rule and reign as My kings and priests, My ambassadors in the earth, representing Me. You belong to Me, and I belong to you. Every care and every weight do I your Father hold, so cast them on Me. You are a child of the King. I reign forever, and I will always be supreme. Remember you are a child of the King.

You don't have to beg me for anything; simply ask. And I will take your request and petition and release it in the timing and purpose for that season. Simply surrender and press past the thoughts in your imagination, and know that I created you for My purpose, for My pleasure, for you to walk out My assignment for your life. Oh, child, hear Me when I say I love you; I look out for you. I want the best for you. So when the enemy comes to you with lies and deceit telling you that I don't care, that I don't love you, or that I left you to fend for yourself, say these words back to him: "It is written, He loves me with an everlasting love (Jeremiah 31:3). It is written, I am the apple of His eye (Zechariah 2:8). It is written, He is the good shepherd (John 10:11)." Receive and believe My word.

Begin to meditate on it day and night, night and day. Let it be written on your heart. Know who you are in Me. Remember you are a child of the King! You belong to My Kingdom. My great host of angels wait for you to speak; pray, and they will move at My very command. Seek Me anytime, anyplace, and anywhere, and I will reveal Myself to you. For you are Mine, and I am yours.

Scriptures for Reflection

Isaiah 46:10

Declaring the end *and* the result from the beginning, And from ancient times the things which have not [yet] been done, Saying, 'My purpose will be established, And I will do all that pleases Me *and* fulfills My purpose.'

Psalm 37:23

The steps of a [good and righteous] man are directed and established by the Lord, And He delights in his way [and blesses his path].

Chapter 6

Come To Me And Know That You Are

Psalm 139:14

I will give thanks *and* praise to You, for I am fearfully and
wonderfully made;
Wonderful are Your works,
And my soul knows it very well.

THE FATHER SPEAKS

Come to Me and know that you are fearfully and wonderfully made.

You are fearfully and wonderfully made.

I say it again until you understand that you are fearfully and wonderfully

made. I called you out of darkness into My marvelous light.

You are My workmanship. You are exquisite.

I love you with an everlasting love. I know when My child is hurting.

I know you believe that I don't care, but that is so far from the truth.

Hear Me when I say I have not forgotten you.

I see you right where you are. I see the tears no one else can see.

I hear the cry of your heart, when no one else can feel the hurt

and the shame and all the pain.

Release it and give it all to Me.

Let Me release you from your captivity. I sing My song over you.

I decree and declare your freedom!

Because whom the Son makes free is free indeed.

Trying to find your worth can be hard when you have felt for so long that you were nothing and had nothing to offer. Growing up, I was always looking for attention, looking for affirmations from a dad who was not there. I remember going through times when I would get my hair done weekly, get my nails done every two weeks, and make sure that I had on the right outfit, thinking that this would make people notice me. They noticed all right, but I was receiving the wrong attention, because my heart was not right. My motives and intentions were wrong. As I tried to find my worth in what other people thought about me, I came to realize that my worth was not going to be found in people. My worth was given to me by the Almighty God. He called me precious and beautiful and the apple of His eye. Having to see my worth through His eyes didn't come easy.

After the sexual abuse, I went through a period of shame and feeling like crap. Yes, crap! That's the only word I can use to describe how I was feeling during that season of my life. I felt like no one would want me, because I was damaged goods. Who could love me and treat me special when all they would see was someone ugly look-ing back at them?

I didn't realize how beautiful I was until I began to spend time with God and He began to tell me what I meant to Him, and I started to believe Him. When you look in the mirror, what do you see? Do you see someone beautiful staring back at you, or do you find flaws or things you would change about yourself that you believe would make you beautiful? That's a huge problem in today's society - people making changes to their appearance because they want to look better or because they see others who they think are gorgeous, and they want to be just like them, whether that means changing their eyes, nose, lips, eyebrows, stomach, or butt. Society is inundated with these like-minded people, because they also don't know their worth.

If they only knew they were created and beautiful to God just the way they are. I am not saying everyone who has a procedure done has self-esteem issues, but I am saying they may not know who they are in Christ. Because once you know, it's like you see yourself in another light.

I remember I was dating this guy, and he was promising to marry me if I would just lose a few pounds. I know that's crazy on so many levels, but I did what any low-self-esteem girl would do. I began to lose the weight. Now you may ask, did I marry that fool? No, I didn't, because God in His love came and saved me before I made one of the worst decisions of my life. I finally realized, "Wait a minute. If I lose the weight so he will finally propose, will he leave me if I gain it back after having kids, or after eating my favorite Blue Bell ice cream?"

Looking back, I realize that was unacceptable, but we do such things for people to accept us. Now today I think I am the greatest thing in God. I see that He made me perfect. He sees me as beautiful, and I am His greatest treasure. As I receive what He says and thinks about me, I am able to walk in confidence and be secure in who I am in Christ.

I COULD TOUCH THE HEAVENS

Above the nice and fluffy white clouds,

above the night's highest shining star,

there You were smiling down on me.

It was like a present waiting to be unwrapped.

The word love sounds so beautiful,

especially when your whole life, you have been searching for

someone to love and someone to love you.

I have found that someone,

and He was right here all along.

He said He would never leave nor forsake me;

that's what I call love.

Back down to earth, where the sun still shines,

I see all these people seeking to find the same love I have found; they

are looking in material things

and other human beings.

They won't find love there.

Only above the nice and fluffy white clouds,

above the night's highest shining star,

there they will find God's love shining down.

The Response from the Beloved

A love song to my beloved. I say these words from my heart. I speak these sayings, for You are my God. I love how You wrap me in Your presence. I love how You sing of my deliverance. You are my love song. You don't question whether or not You will love me. You just do.

Every day I wake up to Your love for me. I wake up to Your peace for me. I wake up to my beloved. No more distractions, no more idols between You and me, for You are my beloved. No one compares to You.

No human could ever measure up to You. Nothing could ever replace You. For You are my beloved. In a world of fairy tales, You are my knight in shining armor. You are my prince on a white horse coming to rescue me and deliver me from the enemy. For You are my beloved, and You mean the world to me.

You said in Your word that You are my husband. You will protect and cover me. You will take care of me. You wash me with Your word. You gave Your very life for me. Now, that's what I call love. You called me Your beloved, and I call You my beloved.

Scriptures for Reflection

John 8:36

So if the Son makes you free, then you are unquestionably free.

Romans 8:1

[*Escape from Bondage*] Therefore there is now no condemnation [no guilty verdict, no punishment] for those who are in Christ Jesus [who believe in Him as personal Lord and Savior].

Romans 12:2

And do not be conformed to this world [any longer with its superficial values and customs], but be transformed *and* progressively changed [as you mature spiritually] by the renewing of your mind [focusing on godly values and ethical attitudes], so that you may prove [for yourselves] what the will of God is, that which is good and acceptable and perfect [in His plan and purpose for you].

Philippians 3:13-14

[13]Brethren, I count not myself to have apprehended: but this one thing I do, forgetting those things which are behind, and reaching forth unto those things which are before, [14]I press toward the mark for the prize of the high calling of God in Christ Jesus. (KJV)

Chapter 7

Come To Me And Cry Out

Psalm 34:17

When *the righteous* cry [for help], the LORD hears And rescues
them from all their
distress *and* troubles.

THE FATHER SPEAKS

Come to Me and cry out and let the tears fall;

Know that I place them in a bottle.

I see the very depth of your soul. I see your pain, hurt, and shame;

I even see your abandonment issues.

I am your Father; I will care for you and speak peace over you.

I am not ashamed of you;

You are my child, and I alone will protect you.

Trust Me and know; be still and wait in My presence.

Listen closely to My voice; I am He Who watches over thee,

Who makes you free;

Now listen intently with your ears and hear Me call your name;

Out of the ashes you will rise and begin to see beauty with your eyes.

I am He that releases thee; I am He that walks on the seas;

I am He that knows everything you try to hold in.

But I say let it out; but I say scream it out;

But I say come to Me with everything!

I can say from experience that I do not like to cry. I felt like I had cried all my life, and I was tired of crying, because I felt like my tears didn't mean anything. But oh, how I was wrong. My tears meant everything to God, so much so that He places them in a bottle. Even now I sometimes struggle with crying out to God, but I remind myself that He sees me right where I am. I believe that our tears are a release for our emotions so that we don't have to feel tensed and stressed in our bodies.

When I have a good cry, I feel so relaxed; it's so freeing for me. When I was growing up, it was implied that tears were a sign of weakness meaning you could not handle the situation or the words that were spoken to you. So I held all my feelings in and never would let anyone see them or know that they even existed—until that precious day Jesus came into my heart, and all that was erased.

The tears flowed freely on that day; it was like a dam had broken, because I was crying uncontrollably. Now I remind myself that I don't have to be strong; that's my Father's job. In my weakness, He is my strength. I don't have to be afraid of being unable to handle a situation or words spoken, because that is correct - I can't in myself, but God can in and through me. I can face any obstacle that is set before me with God.

One night when looking back over my life, I cried out. I was lying on my floor in the dark and praying about the relationship that I didn't have with my natural father. I told the Lord, "All I want is for him to love me; that's it. Show me that he cares or something; anything would do at this point." Growing up in a home without a daddy was hard, but I didn't realize how much this affects a child until I got older. As, I cried and prayed to my Father that night, I just let it all hang out.

I had finally gotten past the unforgiveness in my heart toward my father, but now I thought we were never going to have a relationship. It just didn't seem fair. Then the Lord instructed me to call him and talk to him.

I thought, huh? I wanted to say, "Why do I have to call? He is supposed to be the parent, not me," but I kept that to myself and called him the next day. To my surprise, the conversation went well. I said, "Hello, Dad."

He said, "Hey."

"How are you?" I asked.

He answered, "Fine; how are you doing?"

I said, "Good."

Then we just held the phone. I know it sounds funny, but that was the most my dad and I had talked in eighteen years. Then he asked about my son, and I told him that his birthday was coming up, and then we hung up the phone.

Now to my surprise, the Lord told me to call him back a week later, so I did. The conversation went about the same as the first one, but this time he said, "I sent your son something in the mail for his birthday." I replied, "Uhhh, OK, thank you." Well, like he said, I received a card in the mailbox for my son a couple of days later, and he had even put some money in it for him.

Then the Lord said, "I heard you that night when you were crying to Me about the relationship that you wanted with your dad. He is trying to show you that he loves you and cares." I broke down and cried for a lot of reasons. One reason was that my dad had never sent me anything for my birthday, Christmas, or any other holiday just to let me know that he was thinking about me. But he sent my son something, which meant a lot. This opened up the door for the relationship to be formed that I had so longed to have with him.

That following year, he sent me a birthday card and a Christmas present, and we talked more on the phone. Over the next couple of years, my son and I would travel down to see my dad and spend the weekend with him. It was great to see them playing together. I remember one time my son was playing on his lap. It was great to hear my son say, "Granddad, help me," because he was falling off his lap, and he was pretending that he could not hold on. That brought my heart joy. Even to this day, my son still remembers that incident.

The Lord totally restored me and my father's relationship to where it truly felt like no time was lost. I was even able to be there when he was on his deathbed. I played worship music through the night and slept in the chair next to his bed, praising God for restoration. I have said all this to say that when you cry out to the Lord, He hears your every cry and wants to bring healing and restoration to your life. This was just one of many stories I could tell you of how God heard my cry.

PRESSED DOWN

I was pressed down to a point in my life;

I did not want to go on. I felt down and out and even worthless.

I needed someone to help me;

I needed someone to love me;

I needed someone to change me.

That's when I decided to worship You.

When I was low and broken in two,

You picked me up and turned me around,

and I will be forever grateful to You.

My mind's made up.

My heart is fixed.

I'm ready to serve You all the days of my life.

Dear Lord, use me.

Use me.

The Response from the Beloved

Lord, You see for me. You know the way that I take. You equip me with everything that I need to do Your will. I hear You say, "Go; go out and be My hands and feet. Go out and witness for Me. Be that light they can see."

My passion for You, oh Lord, is great. Let it never be taken away. Let my passion burn. Let it burn until all the dross is removed so that I become pure gold.

Let the fire burn deep until I am totally consumed by Your love for me. Let it burn to the point that it spreads throughout my life, throughout my family, throughout the world.

Scriptures for Reflection

John 12:26

If anyone serves Me, he must [continue to faithfully] follow Me [without hesitation, holding steadfastly to Me, conforming to My example in living and, if need be, suffering or perhaps dying because of faith in Me]; and wherever I am [in heaven's glory], there will My servant be also. If anyone serves Me, the Father will honor him.

James 1:2-4

Consider it nothing but joy, my brothers and sisters, whenever you fall into various trials. Be assured that the testing of your faith [through experience] produces endurance [leading to spiritual maturity, and inner peace]. And let endurance have its perfect result *and* do a thorough work, so that you may be perfect and completely developed [in your faith], lacking in nothing.

Ecclesiastes 7:18

It is good that you take hold of one thing (righteousness) and also not let go of the other (wisdom); for the one who fears *and* worships God [with awe-filled reverence] will come forth with both of them.

Chapter 8

Come To Me And I Will Protect You

Psalm 32:7

You are my hiding place; You, LORD, protect me from trouble;
You surround me with songs *and* shouts of deliverance.

THE FATHER SPEAKS

Come to Me, and I will protect you.

I will hide you under the shadow of My wings.

I will show you the way to go.

I am your high tower.

I am your dwelling place.

Come to Me and know that you are safe in this place.

No harm shall befall you.

Step out into the deep with no fear, anxiety, or worry.

Come and follow Me.

Follow My presence; see the cloud and follow Me.

Let go of everything around you that you have been depending on,
and depend and rely on Me alone.

Trust that I know what I am doing in your life.

Trust that I have you.

Know that I am carrying you to your destiny.

The scripture speaks of God's protection in Psalm 32:7: "You are my hiding place; You, Lord, protect me from trouble; You surround me with songs and shouts of deliverance." My God, this scripture speaks volumes to me in so many ways. When it looks like the enemy is going to win and overtake you, the Lord surrounds you with songs and shouts of deliverance.

The Lord has His people and He protects us from the tactics of the enemy. You see, the enemy is after God's people like never before. He does not want you to make it to the purpose and plans that God has for you, so he fights you on every hand, but know that even when the enemy does this, he plays right into God's plan. "And we know [with great confidence] that God [who is deeply concerned about us] causes all things to work together [as a plan] for good for those who love God, to those who are called according to His plan and purpose" (Romans 8:28 [AMP]).

This tells me that no matter what the enemy tries, no matter what the enemy plans, God can turn it all around to where it works in my favor. Just as He did for Joseph when his brothers threw him in a pit and sold him to foreigners, not knowing that God would use it and turn it around for good. He was exalted to a status just under the king to rule, and he ended up able to provide food not just for his brothers but for the whole nation and other nations around Egypt (Genesis 39:20–23; Genesis 41:38–45).

Like Joseph, I believe all of us have experienced times when we are in a pit and can't see our way out. As an intercessor, I felt like I could pray for other people and watch them get their breakthrough, but when I prayed for myself and my situations, I saw no breakthrough, no change for my own life. I prayed and cried, prayed and cried. During this season God sent different prophets and ministers to minister to my heart. He was letting me know that He heard my heart's cry; He saw every tear that fell. I received a couple of significant words during this season. The first one was this:

The woman of God spoke and said, "You are in the center of God's will; you have so many gifts people don't understand; you don't ever talk about it, but your gifts will make room for you. You are in the center of His will. Even with all the things going on around you like a hurricane, you are in the center of God's will, and you will not be shaken, but you will walk in peace and authority. You will be still and let God fight your battle. Men will see it and glorify God. Take all the anointing in the name of Jesus. So be it. Amen.

The second word I received was this:

God hears your prayers. Don't stop praying. You are a quiet giant. Your prayers matter.

The third one was this:

I love you. Trust Me. I hear your prayers.

What I have come to realize is that God was making me during this season. It was a process. Yes, the word "process"—at first I hated this word so much that I would cringe whenever I heard it. God gave me a great friend who saw my struggle, and she bought me a gift. It was wrapped in a beautiful box. When I opened the box, it was a crystal oyster with a pearl on the inside. She said, "I thought of you when I saw this." The pearl represented something very beautiful and worth a lot of money. But to become that pearl, it had to go through a process. One reason the pearl is worth so much is that not every oyster creates a pearl. This is how a pearl is made, according to www.howstuffworks.com:

> "As the oyster grows in size, its shell must also grow. The **mantle** is an organ that produces the oyster's shell, using minerals from the oyster's food. The material created by the mantle is called **nacre**. Nacre lines the inside of the shell.

> The formation of a natural pearl begins when a foreign substance slips into the oyster between the mantle and the shell, which irritates the mantle. It's kind of like the oyster getting a splinter. The oyster's natural reaction is to cover up that irritant to protect itself. The mantle covers the irritant with layers of the same nacre substance that is used to create the shell. This eventually forms a pearl."

According to Wikipedia:

> "The finest quality natural pearls have been highly valued as gemstones and objects of beauty for many centuries. Because of this, *pearl* has become a metaphor for something rare, fine, admirable and valuable. The most valuable pearls occur spontaneously in the wild, but are extremely rare."

Sometimes I felt like the process was going to kill me. Well, what God was after was a killing of my wants and desires. I had to learn how to trust God in the midst of the craziest circumstances. In the midst of trouble. In the midst of not seeing my way out. I wanted everything in my life to go smoothly without any trouble, without any heartache…the perfect life. The only problem was there is no such thing as the perfect life. We, as believers, will go through hard times, but we have a God Who is right there with us in the midst of trouble. I remember a time when, after having been unemployed for about two years, I finally received a job as a payroll specialist. I had never made this kind of money in my life. I was in my early twenties, and I was so excited.

I was on fire for the Lord and was grateful for the opportunity. When I started working there, I would bring my very big three-translation Bible, so I could read during my lunch break. I know; I know; I was doing too much, but I really just loved His word and wanted to savor every moment I could with the Lord. Unfortunately, all did not go according to plan. I had received this position because a lady was leaving to go to be with her husband. She was supposed to train me for two weeks before she left.

During this time, her circumstances changed, and she no longer needed to leave. This caused a major issue, because now she wanted her job back. Since they had already hired me, they could not let me go. So I stayed, and she stayed until her two weeks were up. But during this time, she did not train me like she was supposed to, because she was upset that I had her job. I didn't find this out until it was too late and she was gone. I began to get called into the manager's office, because the reports I was running were incorrect. Every time I did a report, someone in upper management would complain that it was wrong. One day a coworker called me into the break room and said,

"Shawna, it's like someone is sabotaging your work. I looked over your reports, and something doesn't add up. Let me check your reports before you send them to the managers." So I agreed to let her review them. Now, this was a big help, because I didn't know I was being set up to fail. I ended up taking my reports home to double-check them before I turned them in.

I was stressed out to the max. I was trying to learn a new position that I did not get proper training for, and this was a fast-paced environment. You really didn't have time to miss a step, because managers were depending on you. I had never been in a position like this, so I was learning as I went. I would clock in early to work and work overtime trying to make sure everything was done correctly. I remember one day the manager came to me and said, "You cannot leave until all the accruals are done." She told me to work with my supervisor to get it done. The only problem with this was that I had a kid, and it was a Friday and I already had plans for after work. So I had to rearrange my plans because of work, which made me more stressed. I wanted to do a good job at work, but now my home life was suffering, because I was too tired to do anything with my son when I made it home. I remember waking up, getting him dressed, dropping him off at day care, and then going straight to work. Then I would leave work, pick him up from day care, go home, feed him, get him ready for day care the next day, and put him to bed. Then I would stay up working on my reports so I could make the corrections when I got to work in the morning. This was my life for several months.

Well, this particular Friday, I stayed because I was told to stay and finish the accruals that I never got a chance to finish, and I had already worked a full shift and overtime that week. So I stayed late once again, but when we got to a certain place in the accruals process, the supervisor said I could leave. I ended up going to choir rehearsal that night and walked into praise and worship…I just cried out to God to help me, because I represented Him, and I wanted to show forth His glory on my job. Don't get me wrong; God moved on my job, and I was able to minister to people about Jesus, and people would ask me to pray for them. This was a blessing, but I just didn't know it would be this hard on a job.

Well little did I know after I left work on that Friday, the manager called my supervisor and asked her where I was, and she said, "She left; I sent her home." Well, when I came in the next day, the manager called me into her office and said she was very angry with me, and she was going to fire me because I had disrespected her authority.

Then she said, "But I had a change of heart, because I said to myself, 'She did not do it out of rebellion or spite, but because she was told to leave by her supervisor.'" So I confirmed with her that was correct, and I would have stayed longer if needed by my supervisor. The scripture that came to mind was, "The king's heart is in the hand of the Lord, as the rivers of water: He turneth it withersoever He will." (Proverbs 21:1 Then she said, "Shawna, you have to do better, or I will have to let you go." I left her office feeling overwhelmed and stressed. I felt like I wasn't doing a good job, but I was trying so hard. Well, to make a long story short, a couple of months later, they fired me. What? They said that I could not keep up with the workload. I really didn't understand. I came in early and left late and came in on the weekends, which was not my regular schedule...but I had to let it go.

I was angry for a time, because I was young and didn't realize that I was not just "let go" but fired, until I tried to file for unemployment. The unemployment office sent me a letter stating that I was denied because I had been fired. This shook my world, because I had a kid to take care of, but nevertheless I had to move on. I did everything I knew to do, but it still wasn't enough. I felt like a failure. But God had another plan after I left there. I went to God asking Him to take care of me and my son.

I really didn't know what He wanted me to do until one night He spoke and told me to go back to school. I thought I clearly had not heard Him correctly, but He kept saying, "Go back to school." I said, "For what type of degree plan?" and He said, "Business." I said, "Lord, the only way I would even consider going back to school for business is if I can run my own business." Well, I went to the school and looked at the catalog under business plans, and what do you know? They had a certificate of technology for a one-year program for business entrepreneurs. I said, "OK, Lord, I guess I am going back to school." While I was there, I got a work-study position as I attended school. The lady who hired me after a year wanted to retire and asked me if I wanted her full-time job. I said no out of fear and went on about my day. Then the Lord said to apply. I said, "Lord, I can't do her job," and He said again, "Apply." So I applied, but this didn't come without resistance.

A part-time person who worked in that department was applying for the job too, and when she told me, I thought, "Well, maybe I didn't hear You correctly, Lord, because surely they are going to give the job to her." She had worked there longer, and she wasn't a student worker like me - she was an actual employee. But the Lord said again, "I said apply," so I did. Well, one week before the interviews were to start, the part-time person came to me and said, "I decided to drop out of the running for that position."

I asked why, and she said that she had just decided not to go for it. I was so overwhelmed, because I saw that God wasn't just speaking aimlessly, but He already knew what the outcome would be. Just to let you know, I got the full-time job and worked for over six years in that department. I learned something very vital that day: when you walk in obedience, you can't help but receive all that God has for you. In that time I was able to pray for and minister to a lot of people on that job. It was one of the best jobs I have ever had. I had my own office and was able to use all the gifts and talents the Lord had placed in me for administration.

Since that day I have been given many opportunities to work at different companies, and use the gifts God has graciously blessed me with. The Lord just keeps on blessing me, and I will be forever grateful to Him.

I WAIT

You're the voice of many waters…

You're timeless.

I see myself standing at the door of Your presence.

I enter in, not knowing what to expect

but hoping that great expectation awaits me.

I see the Lord; He's holy.

I see the Lord; He's righteous.

I see the Lord; He is perfect.

I see the Lord in all His majesty.

I wait on You;

I wait on You;

I wait for You to reveal Yourself to me in all Your splendor.

I am overwhelmed by Your greatness,

by Your vastness,

how You surround me with Your presence.

All I know is I am safe here

in Your presence, here in Your presence.

Prayer
Lord Move

Lord, move for them the same way You saw me through; The same way You spoke and calmed all my fears; How I became strong in You; You strengthen me with Your songs.

How You danced over me; How You spoke Your word to me, over and over again. Do the same for them. Amen.

To My Beloved

Under the shadow of My wings shall you abide. My great shelter of protection, My high tower is where you shall be safe, surrounded by My warring angels as you go about your day. Plenty of My words do I speak to guide your way. Move by My word.

I have placed a cloud for you by day and a flaming fire for you by night. Come and abide in Me. Come and sit at My feet. I blanket you with My love.

You are My child, and I am your Father, your protector, your safeguard, your hiding place. So come. So come and let Me wrap you in My loving arms of safety. I am your shield and buckler. I am your exceeding great reward.

Scriptures for Reflection

Psalm 91:1-8

[1]He that dwelleth in the secret place of the most High shall abide under the shadow of the Almighty.

[2]I will say of the LORD, He is my refuge and my fortress: my God; in him will I trust.

[3]Surely he shall deliver thee from the snare of the fowler, and from the noisome pestilence.

[4]He shall cover thee with his feathers, and under his wings shalt thou trust: his truth shall be thy shield and buckler.

[5]Thou shalt not be afraid for the terror by night; nor for the arrow that flieth by day;

[6]Nor for the pestilence that walketh in darkness; nor for the destruction that wasteth at noonday.

[7]A thousand shall fall at thy side, and ten thousand at thy right hand; but it shall not come nigh thee.

[8]Only with thine eyes shalt thou behold and see the reward of the wicked. (KJV)

Chapter 9

Come To Me And Humble Yourself

James 4:10

Humble yourselves [with an attitude of repentance and insignificance] in the presence of the Lord, and He will exalt you [He will lift you up, He will give you purpose].

THE FATHER SPEAKS

Come to Me and humble yourself so you can receive My victory.

Pray and cry out…cry out and pray!

Come to Me and know My presence;

Wait for Me in the stillness of your life.

I know all your faults.

I know all your failures.

I know all your insecurities.

Won't you just come to Me?

I will speak to your desolate places.

I will cause rivers of living waters to flow in your desert place.

I will spring up in the midst of your circumstances.

Come to Me, and you will see…

My splendor, majesty, love, and all My glory.

So humble yourself: what does that really mean? Unfortunately, many people think they are humbled but are not. According to Google the word humble means "having or showing a modest or low estimate of one's own importance." I know you may not believe it, but sometimes we have to be taught humility through the things we suffer. I went through many different types of humbling experiences in my life. I came to an understanding that I have nothing to offer God but a crucified life, one that was sold out to Him and Him alone.

I owe man nothing but to love them. I must be obedient to the One Who saved me from hell and destruction. I remember when I started to help out at a local church for twenty-five dollars a month. I was on food stamps and received child support, but that was it. I remember during that time I didn't understand what God was doing in my life.

But He was teaching me that He was my supply. He was my provision. Whatever I had need of, He was it. I remember crying out to the Lord, asking Him to allow me to just take care of my son. I did not want him to go without, and the amazing thing is he didn't. God was breaking down my life so that I knew He was my only source of hope, my only source of sufficiency.

I had to borrow my mom's car to go to the store, church, and school. During that time I had a dream. I was in church, and a woman of God told me that it had to be this way because of where God was going to take me in my finances. I began to learn obedience during this time and how to listen to the voice of the Lord for my life. I came to understand that when we walk in obedience, God is responsible for the outcome and not us. I came to realize that God just wanted my yes and for me to understand that He was and will be everything that I will ever need.

This was probably one of the most stressful times in my life, because I didn't just have myself to take care of, but I had a little boy to feed and clothe, and I didn't know how I was going to do it. And still I had to feed and clothe myself and try to spend time with my son even though I was feeling low and depressed. I remember I wrote down one day how I was feeling, and it went like this: "I am feeling depressed, because I feel like I cannot take care of me and my son. I do not know which direction to take regarding school. I feel like a failure." God completely restored everything I thought I had lost. He went above and beyond anything I could have ever imagined.

And He keeps blowing my mind every time He makes a way for me. This season taught me that I could not depend on myself for anything - not food, clothing, or even my next breath - but I had to depend on the One Who created me and loved me and had my best interest at heart. People can look at the things that I have now—a car, a house, clothes, and food in my refrigerator—but it hasn't always been like this. I understand it is only by the grace of God that I have what I have. It is all for His glory so that I can tell my story of how He brought me out of poverty and enlarged my territory. These experiences also prepared me for ministry. I understand that it's not on me to do anything or to make something happen, but it is all on God. I just need to walk in obedience to His voice. I don't need to offer my ideas on how I think it should go, but understanding it's His will, His way, His glory.

GOD'S PLAN IS ALWAYS GREATER

God's plan is wonderful.

God's plan is perfect.

God's plan is masterful.

Sometimes you don't understand the situation you're in.

Only know it is the beginning of God's great plan.

To My Beloved

Be mindful of Me. Be sure to do whatever pleases Me. Faith pleases Me; your worship pleases Me. Taking care of the widows and orphans pleases Me. Your praise pleases Me. Your heart toward the poor pleases Me.

Your giving of your time to go to the prisons pleases Me. Your time spent in My presence to hear what I want to say pleases Me. Your living for Me in righteousness pleases Me.

Your believing My word pleases Me. Your obedience pleases Me. Continue to please Me. Continue to give Me pleasure. Continue to follow Me. Continue in My word. Continue to come after Me. Continue to humble yourself before Me.

Continue to run after Me. Continue to trust and believe Me. Continue, for it is I Who causes you to triumph. It is I Who declares My word for your life. It is I Who moves on your behalf. It is I Who sends My angels to watch over you. It is I Who surrounds you with favor as with a shield. It is I…it is I…

Scriptures for Reflection

2 Corinthians 4:7-12

[7]But we have this *precious* treasure [the good news about salvation] in [unworthy] earthen vessels [of human frailty], so that the grandeur *and* surpassing greatness of the power will be [shown to be] from God [His sufficiency] and not from ourselves. [8]We are pressured in every way [hedged in], but not crushed; perplexed [unsure of finding a way out], but not driven to despair; [9]hunted down *and* persecuted, but not deserted [to stand alone]; struck down, but never destroyed; [10]always carrying around in the body the dying of Jesus, so that the [resurrection] life of Jesus also may be shown in our body. [11]For we who live are constantly [experiencing the threat of] being handed over to death for Jesus sake, so that the [resurrection] life of Jesus also may be evidenced in our mortal body [which is subject to death]. [12]So *physical* death is [actively] at work in us, but [spiritual] life [is actively at work] in you.

Psalm 51:17

My [only] sacrifice [acceptable] to God is a broken spirit; A broken and contrite heart [broken with sorrow for sin, thoroughly penitent], such, O God, You will not despise.

Proverbs 3:34

Though He scoffs at the scoffers *and* scorns the scorners, Yet He gives His grace [His undeserved favor] to the humble [those who give up self-importance].

Proverbs 11:2

When pride comes [boiling up with an arrogant attitude of self-importance], then come dishonor *and* shame, But with the humble [the teachable who have been chiseled by trial and who have learned to walk humbly with God] there is wisdom *and* soundness of mind.

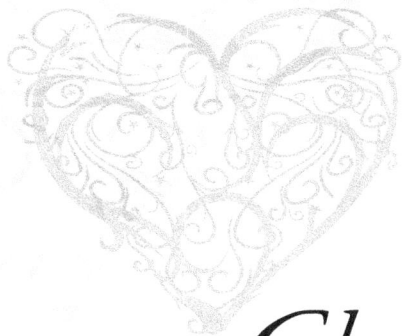

Chapter 10

Come To Me With Your Whole Heart

Jeremiah 29:11-13

For I know the plans *and* thoughts that I have for you,' says the LORD, 'plans for peace *and* well-being and not for disaster, to give you a future and a hope. [12] Then you will call on Me and you will come and pray to Me, and I will hear [your voice] *and* I will listen to you. [13] Then [with a deep longing] you will seek Me *and* require Me [as a vital necessity] and [you will] find Me when you search for Me with all your heart.

THE FATHER SPEAKS

Come to Me with your whole heart, and I will guide your

footsteps. I will lead you on My path of righteousness.

I will lend My ear to you to hear your petitions and requests.

I will guide you to Me.

In My very presence, you will see, with your eyes wide open, My

decrees. My words that I speak over you.

What I declare is true!

Run after Me with all your heart and know that I am

He that surrounds you with peace,

That speaks to you in clarity.

Pursue My ways, My character, My heart!

I remember the day God told me to give Him my whole heart. I didn't quite know what that meant. I thought, "OK, here You go," but I didn't understand what He was really asking for. It was a time when I wanted to hold on to something, because I felt like my world was caving in. I wanted some kind of comfort and was looking for someone, anyone, to ease my pain. I looked for people, places, and things. God was asking me to lay my family, job, school, church, bills, and anything I was holding on to (besides Him), before Him.

When you lay down these things before Him, it's you releasing your will, your way, and your outcome of the situation. No more control, truly trusting God with it. You are telling God, "I don't know what to do, and even if I think I know, it still may not be Your way." It means letting Him have it all.

Your whole heart…those are words some people still don't comprehend. According to the Merriam-Webster dictionary, the word "whole" means, "having all its proper parts or components; complete, unmodified; constituting the total sum or undiminished entirety."

The best way I can explain it is for you to imagine an apple pie, half of which has been eaten. This is not considered a whole apple pie; it is some but not all. We treat God like this. We come to Him with half of our heart, and we hold on to the rest. We say, "God, fix this right here, which is what I am presenting to You a piece of my heart," and He doesn't want a piece; He wants it all. You give Him your hurts and even your dreams and aspirations. You give Him everything, whether you want to be married and have kids or whether you want to become a famous doctor traveling the world. This is all apart of you—your ideas, your desires, anything that you could dream; that's what He wants.

When you bring this before Him, He will begin to speak concerning these very issues of your heart. He will give you direction; He will speak healing, and He will give correction. Whenever you go through anything, bring it to God. Let Him know how you feel. Let Him know that it hurts. Let Him know that you don't understand. Let Him know you don't have any words to say because you feel numb on the inside. Let Him know: talk to Him, and He will listen to you. It doesn't always have to be audible; sometimes you may not even open your mouth, but you are speaking to Him from your heart, mind, and soul. Give Him your whole heart.

There is such peace, a stillness and calmness that happens when you choose to give it all to Him, because it puts you in a place of having to trust Him with everything. Yes, trust Him; oh, how I know it can be hard to do this, because we still want the outcome the way we want it and not necessarily the way He has planned it for us. But we have to believe His word. Romans 8:28 states, "And we know [with great confidence] that God [who is deeply concerned about us] causes all things to work together [as a plan] for good for those who love God, to those who are called according to His plan and purpose."

HAVE YOUR WAY IN ME

Have Your way. In total surrender, I give You my life. I give You my all. I give You everything I can muster up inside. I choose to surrender all. I choose to lay it all down at Your feet. I choose to give it to You—everything that I am. All that I possess, everything that I carry, I choose to give it to You. "Lord, have Your way," is what I am saying. "Lord, get Your glory," is what I am saying. "Lord, do what only You can do," is what I am saying. Lord, have Your way; have Your way in me.

Through the brokenness, through the heartache, through the pain, through the struggle, have Your way, oh God, in me. You chose me before the foundations of the world. You created me in my mother's womb. You knit me together and fashioned me for a great purpose. So Lord, have Your way; have Your way in me. It doesn't feel good; the pain seems unbearable at times. The hurt consumes my heart, but Lord, have Your way, have Your way in me.

I choose to lay aside every weight, every sin, everything that holds me back from You, everything that keeps me from walking in obedience to Your word, everything that keeps me and impedes my progress toward the Almighty God, toward the Savior of the world, toward the King of kings, toward the Almighty. Lord. Have Your way; have your way in me.

Father, I renounce anything that I have taken on as truth that is a lie. I renounce any deception that I have believed that is not truth, that is not Your word. And I choose to believe, and I take up Your word this day. I take up what You say about me this day. I believe what You say about me this day and forever. Lord, have Your way in me.

I know we cry out, "Lord, have Your way in me," and sometimes we mean it, and sometimes we don't even know what we are asking. But for You to truly have Your way in me, I know I must—I must surrender. I must—I must yield. I must—I must give it all to You. I must choose to trust and believe. I must cry out to You. There is no other way for You to have Your way in me unless I give You me. Unless I give You all of me.

The Response from the Beloved

Lord, I come to You as You ask me to. I come and lay down everything that I am. Every gift, every agenda. I come to You with my family, my possessions.

I come and give You all my heart, holding nothing back. Be pleased with me. Oh God, I choose to give You everything. I come to You releasing my past hurts, my pains, and all my desires. Even though I can't see You, I choose to come and acknowledge You, Your presence in my life.

I come to You. You're worth more to me than anything in this world. I come and incline my ear to hear Your voice so my soul can live. (Isaiah 55 [KJV]). I give You all of me; I am totally free in You. Lord, You made me, and I belong to you. So I come to You.

Scriptures for Reflection

Mathew 6:19-21

[19]"Do not store up for yourselves [material] treasures on earth, where moth and rust destroy, and where thieves break in and steal. [20]But store up for yourselves treasures in heaven, where neither moth nor rust destroys, and where thieves do not break in and steal; [21]for where your treasure is, there your heart [your wishes, your desires; that on which your life centers] will be also.

Isaiah 48:17

This is what the LORD, your Redeemer, the Holy One of Israel says, "I am the LORD your God, who teaches you to profit (benefit), Who leads you in the way that you should go.

Chapter 11

Come To Me And Be Renewed

Psalm 119:37

Turn my eyes away from vanity [all those worldly, meaningless
things that distract—let Your priorities be mine],
And restore me [with renewed energy] in Your ways.

Psalm 138:3

On the day I called, You answered me;
And You made me bold *and* confident with
[renewed] strength in my life.

THE FATHER SPEAKS

Come to Me and be renewed, be refreshed in My presence.

I lift up My standard against the floods of the enemy. Be refreshed and renewed.

Know that I am on your side.

I fight for you; the battle is not yours.

Be refreshed, be renewed; I am always watching over you.

I know the way that you take.

I have ordered your steps in righteousness.

I say go and be at peace.

I say arise and let your light shine.

I say go and flow in Me.

Go, arise, My child, and walk toward Me.

I am the lifter of your head.

During the night season, one of the biggest things we need is to be renewed. Psalm 119:37 says, "Turn my eyes away from vanity [all those worldly, meaningless things that distract—let Your priorities be mine], And restore me [with renewed energy] in Your ways." So many of us get caught up with distraction. Distractions cause us to lose focus. In the Merriam-Webster dictionary, the word "distraction" means, "an object that directs one's attention away from something else: mental confusion." If we are not careful, we will find ourselves entangled with the cares of this world and lose the true meaning of why we are here, which is to give God glory in fulfilling our purpose and assignments.

When I began to focus only on the Lord, He began to restore me. The pressures of this world came to weigh me down, but God wanted me at peace and walking in freedom. When I began to worship, I forgot about my pain, hurt, anger, and anything else that was going on in my life. I began to think on Him and His goodness, how He was God all by Himself. The angels surround His throne and cry, "Holy, Holy, Holy." I thought about how He was the God over all the nations, how He was mighty in battle and never lost.

When I began to think of His majesty, His righteousness, His holiness, I began to forget about all my problems, and I fell down and worshipped Him, because He was God Almighty. He was a big God Who created the whole world, the universe, the stars in the sky, and all the planets. He was God Who held the nations in His hand. He was in total control. He was supreme, and there is no one beside Him, and there never will be. He is the ruler of all. The sun rises and sets at His command. He holds back the waters and keeps them from taking over the land. He makes promises that He keeps. He never fails. I would open my mouth and begin to sing praises to an almighty, all-knowing, and ever-present God. As I opened my mouth, the cares, worries, frustrations, and fears began to leave. Then I would begin to hear the Lord speak to my heart, letting me know that He saw me right where I was and that He was in control of everything.

After crying out in worship, I would just lie there in His presence and receive any and everything that I needed in that precious moment. When I arose from my posture, it felt like the weight of the world was lifted off my shoulders. Psalm 138:3 (KJV) became very real to me that day: "On the day I called, You answered me; And You made me bold and confident with renewed strength in my life."

I encourage you to begin to open your mouth and speak from your heart. Say, "thank You, Lord," from a real place of worship and praise.

You are the God who was with Daniel in the lion's den.

You are the God who is the great I am.

You were with David when he fought Goliath,

and You are the one who saved Israel out of the Philistines' hand.

You are the one who was with Moses

to deliver the children of Israel out of Pharaoh's snare.

You are the God who was with Elijah

when 850 false prophets fell.

You are the God who was with Hannah

when she asked You for a son, and she gave birth to the prophet Samuel.

You are the God who was with Joshua

when they walked around the city, and the walls came tumbling down.

You are the God who was with Queen Esther

as she went before the king to request that he save the Jews.

You are the same God who is with me through and through.

Prayer

Let Your Worshippers Come

Lord, I pray for a spirit of worship and praise and adoration to consume those who are reading this right now. They will begin to release the sound of praise and worship. Let the melodies of heaven rise up in their bellies. Let them begin to flow by Your spirit. Let them begin to hear the sound that You carry.

Let the winds blow now; let change come to their atmosphere now. Let them sense You moving on their behalf. Let them rise up and bless Your name. Let the worshippers arise and cry out, "Holy, Thou art holy. Righteous, Thou art righteous. From everlasting to everlasting, Thou art God, King, ruler of everything."

You reign for all eternity, in the brilliance of Your splendor and majesty. How majestic are Your ways. The love, grace, mercy, and judgment that flow from Your throne encapsulates Who You are, everlasting Father, Prince of peace.

All that You are encompasses me. Be glorified, oh great King. Be high and lifted up, oh great and Holy Majesty. We reverence You for all that You are. Reveal to me more of Who You are, Almighty God, Who reigns forever and ever. Amen.

Scriptures for Reflection

Exodus 24:16

The glory *and* brilliance of the LORD rested on Mount Sinai, and the cloud covered it for six days. On the seventh day God called to Moses from the midst of the cloud.

Exodus 40:34

[*The Glory of the LORD*] Then the cloud [the Shekinah, God's visible, dwelling presence] covered the Tent of Meeting, and the glory *and* brilliance of the LORD filled the tabernacle.

Luke 2:14

"Glory to God in the highest [heaven], And on earth peace among men with whom He is well-pleased."

Chapter 12

Come To Me And Know

Exodus 3:14

God said to Moses, "[a]I AM WHO I AM"; and He said, "You shall say this to the Israelites, 'I AM has sent me to you.'"

THE FATHER SPEAKS

Come to Me, and know that I am God.

I hold the enemy at bay.

I speak victory and life over you.

You are My prized possession.

I cannot and will not fail.

Come to Me with all your fears.

Come to Me with all your cares.

Know that I am He Who sees.

My Son Jesus intercedes for you at My right hand

So that you will make it through.

I have you written in the palm of My hand.

I wait…

I wait…

And I wait…

For you to come to Me.

In the night seasons, there may be times when you become depressed and feel all alone, like no one cares. You wish people could see you on the inside — the hurt, the pain, and the shame — but they don't. When I was in my night season, one of the darkest places in my life, I felt totally abandoned, like I was left alone to carry my burdens with no help from anyone. I would cry in my bed in the middle of the night, crying out to God from within, because I could not express with words how I felt, and nothing would come out of my mouth.

I screamed from within, praying that He heard me and that He cared and at least saw me in the state I was in. I cried, cried, and cried. I felt no relief for that moment. The next thing I remember is waking up to my alarm clock…but I didn't even remember falling asleep. So I would get up by the grace of God and go to work, take care of my son, go to church, and so on. I was pressing through my emotions, fears, and uncertainty, not knowing what to expect next.

I found myself closing myself off from people, family, and friends, because I felt that if I tried to explain how I felt or what I was going through, I would not be able to articulate the pain and the anger. But I would hear the Lord say, "Come to Me and spend time with Me." I would find myself getting up out of my bed and walking slowly to my prayer closet. I would sit down, and tears would begin to fall; I would begin to feel the stress leaving my shoulders and neck. I remember wanting to run and hide from His presence because I felt like He didn't care, but that was far from the truth. He cared very much, because I was His child.

He cared about how I was feeling and the situation I was in. He cared about my hurts, pains, and struggles within. Every time I stepped out and went to Him when He called me, it never failed. He would minister to my heart. He would begin with the words "I love you," which in return would make me cry even more. He would say, "I know what I am doing…trust Me. I see you right where you are." Then He would speak a scripture, and I would pick up my Bible and turn to it. This is one of many scriptures He spoke to me: "Even to your old age I am He, And even to your advanced old age I will carry you; I have made you, and I will carry you; Be assured I will carry you and I will save you" (Isaiah 46:4 [AMP]).

This is when I realized that if I sat still long enough in His presence, He would minister to my heart right where I was. During this fifteen-year span of going in and out of all the turbulence and frustration, there were some praiseworthy moments and glimpses of light that the Lord would allow in my life to encourage my soul and to bring peace to the raging war within and around me. Praise and worship brought me through the most difficult times in my life. There were moments when God would just show up on the scene and move on my behalf so that I knew it was nobody but Him. I thank God for my friends who prayed for me and kept me before the throne of God. I used to care what people would say and what people thought about me, but no more.

God is my high tower and my exceeding great reward. He is my buckler and strength and a very present help in the time of trouble. I have come to realize that I can have peace and rest in

Him no matter what heartache or disappointments I face. I choose to go to Him in the night seasons of my life, and He will instruct my heart.

It's during these times I went to Him that depression had to go. Suicidal thoughts had to leave. Anger had to subside, and forgiveness was allowed to reign in my life. I would be so overwhelmed by His love for me and others that I could no longer stay in the places where I was comfortable. He healed my heart and showed me grace.

Sing to the Lord, the mighty king.

Praise His name; worship before His throne.

Acknowledge that the Lord is God.

Lift all your praises up to Him.

Praise the Lord, our God,

for He is the supreme king.

The Lord is great.

Come, let us praise His holy name.

He made us and not we ourselves.

For holy is He…

Holy. Holy. Holy.

Prayer
Depression Has to Go!

Lord, I ask that You deliver my brother and my sister from the spirit of depression this very hour. Lord, heal the wounds of their hearts. Let them know that You are not finished with them yet. For You know the thoughts that You think toward them, thoughts of peace and not of evil, to give them an expected end. They do not have to fear tomorrow, for You said in Your word, "It is the Lord who goes before you; He will be with you. He will not fail you or abandon you. Do not fear or be dismayed" (Deuteronomy 31:8).

Let them begin to encourage themselves just like David did. For those who are overwhelmed by the cares of this world—allow them to begin to release all their cares to You, casting them all upon You, because You care for them. Allow them to see that You will give them beauty for their ashes. This is not the end; there is still more for them to do. They will not give up, but they will press toward the mark of the high calling in Christ Jesus.

I speak peace over their minds right now, in the name of Jesus. They have sound minds in You, Lord. They will not lose their minds, because their minds belong to You. No more feeling depressed; no more feeling alone. God is there with you. God is our refuge and strength [mighty and impenetrable], a very present and well-proved help in trouble (Psalm 46:1). So let the tears fall; let them flow, because He puts them in a bottle. Amen.

To My Beloved

My Kingdom is where I called you to live from. Your place is in Me. Your dwelling is right here with Me. Remember the day I saved you? At that moment, all My promises were yours. At that moment, every sin was forgiven, and the sting of death was no longer your portion. I am yours, and you are Mine. You belong to Me.

There is no greater victory than the day My son Jesus laid down His life and rose with all power in His hand. No greater triumph, no greater love. I burn with love for you. I surround you with My grace. You awake every morning with My new mercies.

Go forth and shine for Me. Go forth and be who I called you to be. Go forth and experience in this very hour My plans for your life. Go forth and live out the calling I placed on your life. Don't let what people say or do hold you back. Don't let the looks or the stares cause you to fear or question My words that I speak to you and over you.

Let not one of them impede My design for you. What can mere humankind do to you? Go forth and be! Go forth and do all My good pleasure.

Scriptures for Reflection

Deuteronomy 10:21

He is your praise *and* glory; He is your God, who has done for you these great and awesome things which you have seen with your own eyes.

2 Samuel 22:4

"I call on the LORD, who is worthy to be praised, And I am saved from my enemies.

1 Chronicles 16:9

Sing to Him, sing praises to Him; Speak of all His wonders.

1 Chronicles 16:25

For great is the LORD, and greatly to be praised; He is also to be feared [with awe-filled reverence] above all gods.

Psalm 21:13

Be exalted, LORD, in Your strength; We will sing and praise Your power.

Psalm 22:3

But You are holy, O You who are enthroned in [the holy place where] the praises of Israel [are offered].

Psalm 28:7

The LORD is my strength and my [impenetrable] shield; My heart trusts [with unwavering confidence] in Him, and I am helped; Therefore my heart greatly rejoices, And with my song I shall thank Him *and* praise Him.

Chapter *13*

Come To Me And Watch

Psalm 5:3

In the morning, O LORD, You will hear my voice;
In the morning I will prepare [a prayer and a sacrifice] for You and
watch *and* wait [for You to speak to my heart].

THE FATHER SPEAKS

Come to Me and watch the gifts begin to flow in My presence.

See all that I can do when you just simply come to Me.

I will unlock the destiny, purpose, and plan I have for your life.

Go through the open doors I place before you.

Follow My guidance and the leading of My spirit.

Come to Me and know My word.

Speak My word in this season of your life.

Come to Me and walk and talk with Me.

Bring Me your burdens and cares and watch Me move for you.

Watch Me split your Red Sea and hold back the water at your

Jordan. Just watch Me!

I remember when I was sitting in church one Sunday morning worshipping Him through song, and He began to speak.

"I know you're not worthy of the plans that I have for your future, but I have decided to release you into it. So no longer not worthy but purpose and destiny. So then you must forget the former things and not even consider the things of old, because now it springs forth." Back in 2005 God said my weakness is where He desires me, because His strength in His presence is where He wants me to be. God said give it all to Him.

It's like I see myself laying down everyone who is in my life or has touched my life in any way before Him; laying my job, school, money, car, house, husband, any and everything before Him and following Him and Him alone, not what the world thinks I should have or what I should do, but following the Almighty God and looking to Jesus in everything.

In July 2005 I received a word from the Lord, "The promises that I have told you are coming to pass. I am placing a rod in your back, so you can stand. You will come forth in your season; you will come forth. I haven't forgotten you. I see you in the secret place; the place no one else can see you, but I see you. I am turning around your situation.

I am giving you ears to hear my voice — you will hear Me like never before. Rejoice for what I am doing in your life. Don't worry about your family situation because I got it. Lift up your head." Then He spoke in 2006—"You may need something in your life, but do you need it more than Me," says the Lord. One of the most profound statements God has ever told me in my life was,

"When you don't know which way I am taking you, just know that I am with you."

FINISH

I hear the Lord say, "Finish."

I hear Him say, "Finish.

Run the race before you.

Don't give up, and don't give in,

but finish to the end.

Finish for My glory...

Finish, and tell the story

of how I was with you until the end.

Tell of all the victories and triumphs I gave you.

Speak of the peace that surrounded you.

Tell them how I carried you and surrounded you with hope.

How I encouraged your heart and how I spoke gladness.

I hear the Lord say again, Finish."

Prayer
Fear No More

Lord, I come against the spirit of fear and intimidation. I come against the mind-set that is afraid to move forward to receive everything that You have for them. That paralyzing fear must leave in the name of Jesus.

Lord, I ask that they receive Your perfect love and that they will walk in love. I speak peace to their turmoil and surrounding situations. I speak peace to their minds and every thought that is trying to bombard them.

I thank You that they will begin to walk in obedience according to Your word and surrender everything You are asking of them. In Jesus name, Amen.

To My Beloved

Don't hold back the dreams I placed inside you. Don't hold back the gifts I created in you. Don't hold back the destiny I have for you. No longer will you hold back My words I speak to you. I see the floodwaters held up behind your walls.

Let go and release the flow. Release My anointing into the world. Release My patience, loving-kindness, and compassion to those who don't see. To the ones the devil has blinded and has held back by fear.

Release the sound of My anointing. Release the sound of My unfailing love. Let the waters break forth and let them cover the whole earth. The sound of My winds of change, the winds of newness and freshness blow.

The words from My mouth have been released to the earth to go and perform My good pleasure—walk in it; stand in it; live in it. The winds of Me.

Scriptures for Reflection

Hebrews 12:1

[*Jesus,the Example*] Therefore, since we are surrounded by so great a cloud of witnesses [who by faith have testified to the truth of God's absolute faithfulness], stripping off every unnecessary weight and the sin which so easily *and* cleverly entangles us, let us run with endurance *and* active persistence the race that is set before us,

1 Corinthians 9:24

Do you not know that in a race all the runners run[their very best to win], but only one receives the prize? Run [your race] in such a way that you may seize the prize *and* make it yours!

Galatians 5:7

You were running [the race] well; who has interfered *and* prevented you from obeying the truth?

Philippians 2:16

holding out *and* offering to everyone the word of life, so that in the day of Christ I will have reason to rejoice greatly because I did not run [my race] in vain nor labor without result.

HIS CONCLUSION

Come to Me and give Me you…

All of you…

Every part of you…

From the inside out;

Laying down your gifts and talents at my feet.

Come to Me in humility.

I give you all of Me, so give Me all of you,

So My glory can be seen.

I hold nothing back from you…

No, I hold nothing back from you,

So hold nothing back from Me.

Let your light shine for Me,

So that people will be drawn to Me.

Give Me all the glory!

As you go through your night seasons, God wants you to come to Him. Understand that He created you for His glory and He knows what He is doing. There were days I came in and threw my purse and bags down at the front door and ran to my place with Him and He met me there every time. Don't wait; go to Him because He cares.

When you're scared and don't understand, know this, "I am with you," He said. During every season of my life I had to trust Him with the outcome. I had to trust Him at His word. I had to know that God knew what He was doing. In every pain I felt and in every victory I had, He was right there. 'Come to Me' are three words that carry so much weight. They are words of safety.

Time and time again the Lord showed up in my desolate places and brought me out. My prayer for you is that you allow the Lord to minister to your heart during the hardest times in your life. When you go to Him you will see the turnaround for your life. Even if you don't see it right away, please know that He is for you. He wants to see you healed, set free, and delivered. This book was written with you in mind. "Come to Me" says the Lord, and watch your life change right before your eyes.

Come
To Me

Come
To Me

To learn more about the Come to Me book series by Shawna Prince, or to read sample chapters, log on to the website: www.ComeToMeSeries.com.

Come
To Me

Come
To Me

Come
To Me

Come
To Me

Come
To Me

Come
To Me

Come
To Me

www.ingramcontent.com/pod-product-compliance
Lightning Source LLC
Chambersburg PA
CBHW032048090426
42744CB00004B/125